UNITED STATES UTOPIA

(How To Improve and Enhance the United States of America and its Society)

By

Merrell D. Wilson

UNITED STATES UTOPIA

(How To Improve and Enhance the United States of America and its Society)

First Edition

ISBN 978-1-7325851-2-6

UNITED STATES UTOPIA

(How To Improve and Enhance the United States of America and its Society)

Dedication Page

This Book is being committed to paper in July of 2018; even though it has been in the author's mind to write for many years. It is thus 242 years after the founding of the United States on July 4, 1776. Hopefully the United States will last 250 or more years; but without implementing many of the changes as envisioned by the author in this manuscript, unfortunately, he has his doubts that the country will survive as it is currently constituted.

The author Considers the Ideas in this small book to be more important than it's organization and/or 'prettying up' and as it is a sort of 'Bucket List' book; so he will leave any beautiful revisions of it for the second and future editions.

UNITED STATES UTOPIA

(How To Improve and Enhance the United States of America and its Society)

You may disagree with the solutions and remedies in the book; but that is irrelevant, unless you have solutions and remedies of your own which are superior.

UNITED STATES UTOPIA

(How To Improve and Enhance the United States of America and its Society)

Preface

Those who want the ideas of United States Utopia in a Nutshell should consult the Epilogue where they are stated in a more concise manner.

The author has observed the ills of society his whole life; and these suggestions and measures are the actions and means that he finds necessary to rectify the unfortunate circumstances that many people find themselves in; in life, many times through no fault of their own......except for bad luck.

One might say that it is a person's own fault that they find themselves Homeless, Bankrupt with no resources, addicted to Drugs, or whose parents were killed in an auto accident, or they feel forced to commit crimes to obtain food and shelter. But that is begging the question with no solutions or remedies.

The Solutions and remedies below provide for want of a better term, a Safety Net, to catch Citizens in, when Circumstances have dealt them severe blows.

It is expected that implementation of these Solutions and Remedies would; in the end, Reduce Crime, End Drug Addiction, End the Exploitation of Men Women and Children; and provide them a means to Climb back up the Ladders of Life to Become Productive Citizens. Thus; all Citizens of the Republic would know that; worse come to worse, they would still have opportunities to pull themselves back up by their Boot-Straps......!!

UNITED STATES UTOPIA

(How To Improve and Enhance the United States of America and its Society)

With the Reductions in Crime, Reductions in Drug Addiction, and Reductions in the Exploitation of Men, Women, and Children; the assumed 'Cost' of the Programs would be more than 'Paid' for by the return of all Citizens to a more Productive Life and reduction in the cost of taking care of individuals who would require hospitalization, and remedial or psychiatric or rehabilitation care.

UNITED STATES UTOPIA

(How To Improve and Enhance the United States of America and its Society)

Contents

UNITED STATES UTOPIA

(How To Improve and Enhance the United States of America and its Society)

Education

The Current Educational System in the United States is barely adequate to produce good productive citizens. In a lot of cases; graduates are produced lacking basic social graces, with no idea what they are going to do in life to earn a living, and only rudimentary educational skills to figure out how to make their way in life. Therefore; it is clear that the educational system has to be improved and enhanced.

These Skill sets below need to be taught in addition to the current educational mix.

Everyone must learn how to Dance Several types of Dances. Therefore schools will need a Dance Instructor.

(How To Improve and Enhance the United States of America and its Society)

Everyone must learn the social graces of meeting and greeting people and the ordinary manners you need in social occasions. Therefore schools will need a Social Graces Instructor.

Everyone should learn Financial methods of savings and investment and skills necessary to run a Business. Therefore schools will need a Financial Instructor.

Everyone should learn methods of self defense therefore boxing and other means of protecting oneself should be taught. Therefore schools will need self defense instructors.

A means of resolving disputes between individuals needs to be initiated so that these do not devolve into actual dangerous unsupervised fights. I recommend a form of balance pole fights in which individuals try to knock each other off of narrow ledges by pushing them off balance with poke poles. Anyone winning the contest three out of 5 times would be deemed to be the winner. Of course the individuals, poles and floor onto which they fall would be padded so as to prevent the individuals from sustaining serious injury.

Everyone should have a Sport and a Club and be on a Team or in a Group. Additional sports which might be included are Volleyball, Lacrosse, Epee Fencing, Chess, Astronomy etc. additional Coaches will be needed for these for the Sports and Clubs. The same people can't be on every team or Club; so a person would be restricted to no more than 2 sports and/or 2 clubs. Thus a boy might be on the football and basketball team; but not on the track team. Or a boy might be on the Chess and

Astronomy Club; but not on the Debate Team. Coaches would be allowed to choose their players as it is now; however the Administrators would have the final say as to which teams or clubs a person could participate in; so as to make all sports and clubs representative of the entire school population.

Guidance Counseling. Everyone in Middle and High School would be Required to meet with their Guidance Counselor once a month to Determine their future Objectives to Further their Education and/or their Plans for earning a Living after High School. It is clear therefore that schools will have to hire more guidance Counselors.

Psychological Counseling. Students getting in trouble would have to be reviewed once a year in psychological counseling; to see if some help should be provided in that area.

Students who got in trouble regularly; would have to be reviewed more often. It is therefore clear that schools would have to have a staff of psychologists.

The Government would have to provide the Funding for all of the New Instructors and Guidance Personnel, and Psychologists necessary to be added to the school systems in the United States.

Remedial Education across the board for Elementary, Middle School, High School, College, and Graduate School should be initiated. It should be possible to earn Certification, GEDs, and Degrees without attending the standard schools, if necessary, to Supplement the Standard educational system.

In order to facilitate this; the US Government should implement educational programs with the most highly qualified instructors. Competitions would be done to determine the best Instructors for each Course of Instruction and then they would be put on TV and Taped.

A Home Table-top electronic 'cable' box or Wi-Fi box would connect each home's TV to the educational course the student would need to be remediated in. The student would be enrolled and given a student identification number as well as a Course Logon ID. To verify the student's home attendance; the student would be required to enter his student identification number every now and then to verify his 'attendance' at home with the course by means of a controller. Tests would; of course, be given to verify that the student had grasped the course material and grades would determine if the student had passed the course.

Passing the Course would be given accreditation by the government for covering the course material and the local schools , Colleges, and Universities would have to give the student credit for passing that particular course; also. The government would insure that the electronic 'cable' or Wi-Fi would have connection to the Internet so that each home in a city would be able to connect to all of the courses.

Thus it would be possible to earn a Diploma in GED, Grade School, Middle School, High School, College Degree, Graduate Degree, etc. if that was necessary, without attending the schools. In general; though, it would usually be necessary to attend a school to get in the necessary social skills, life skills, and physical education; although these might be waived depending on the disabilities or problems with attending the local schools.

The 'cable' box or Wi-Fi box would be provided free to all homes requesting it. It would probably be restricted to the educational channels and courses. In this way; even if a student couldn't attend the regular schools or needed remedial instruction in a grade or course; it would be possible for him to make up the grade and/or course in his free, evening, or weekend time. Courses could be saved at whatever each location a student had stopped the course; so that their instruction could proceed at the student's own pace.

Digital Bill of Rights

It is apparent from the current Digital Age; which the Founding Fathers of the United States couldn't have Foreseen; that a new Digital Bill of Rights needs to be crafted as an Amendment to the Constitution and passed by the required number of state assemblies to add it to our Constitution as the original Bill of Rights was added. This is a first draft of such a Digital Bill of Rights for the United States.

Exceptions to most of the Digital Bill of Rights will have to be made for Warrants issued by a Court of Law to remedy Criminal Activity, Terrorism Activity, Saboteur Activity, Spy Activity, Illegal Funding Activity, Illegal Money Laundering or Illegal Manipulation of Markets, Fraud Activity, and/or any other Activities

UNITED STATES UTOPIA

(How To Improve and Enhance the United States of America and its Society)

Deemed to be Illegal or Treasonous against the United States or Activities Tending towards the Breakdown of the Society of the United States; including Criminal Activity for which the Citizen has been arrested by the police....

Digital Rights of the U.S. Citizen.

Citizens have an automatic copyright of their Digital or Photographic appearance. It cannot be used without the citizens written and signed permission.

Citizens have an automatic copyright of their Digital or Photographic Signatures. It cannot be used without the citizens written and signed permission.

Citizens have an automatic copyright of the Digital or Photographic appearance of their personal property. It cannot be used without their written and signed permission.

Citizens have an automatic copyright of their Fingerprints, DNA, Body Parts. They cannot be used, or seized, or converted to other uses without their written and signed permission.

Citizens have a right Not to be tracked in their movements by electronic mediums without their written and signed permission. This applies to tracking by means of maps and gps coordinates and/or any other kinds of tracking to determine their location and/or internet location. This information cannot be used without their written and signed permission.

Citizens have a right not to be tracked in their searches upon the internet by electronic means without their written and signed permission. The information cannot be used without their written and signed permission.

Citizens have a right not to have their personal information stored in a database without their written and signed permission. This information cannot be used without their written and signed permission.

Citizens have a right to their email addresses, ISPs, Websites, and Digital Locations. This information cannot be stored or utilized without their written and signed permission.

Citizens have a right to their personal emails, text messages, 'Tweets' , Photographs or Selfies that they have sent or generated to any restricted or short list of correspondents.

The Correspondents would not have the right to publicly advance or re-send such communications without the permission of the sender. The exception would be that such emails, etc. which are released into a public forum would no longer be protected.

Citizens have the right not to be subjected to cookies merely for visiting a website. Websites should be upfront about requiring users to become 'members' by logging in and in this way they can utilize their cookies with their 'members'. A Website is either Public or it is not. If it is Public; then it has no right to install cookies on the public who merely browse the website.

Citizens have the right not to have their searches on the internet individually kept as data. If a search engine wants to keep personal data on searches; then it would have to have the Citizen join that search engine as a 'member'. Surreptitious keeping of search data would be illegal. Search engines could keep data on individual searches if they had an established method for paying the individual for his search data and the citizens had given written and signed permission for them to do so.

All Such permissions must be by written form with written or Digital Signatures provided before the Citizen gives away the right of any other entity to utilize the above information. A checkbox or email address provided and/or continued usage of a website would be considered an insufficient right by another entity to utilize the information without the written or Digital Signature provided by the Citizen.

UNITED STATES UTOPIA

(How To Improve and Enhance the United States of America and its Society)

Plus other Digital Rights as may be added later to this first draft of Digital Rights.

Social Security and other Government Entitlement Programs

In order to prevent the oft-mentioned Bankruptcy or Reduction of or Failure of the Social Security Program; it will be necessary to increase the social security deduction in paychecks by a small amount and with the funds thus generated to buy stocks or other securities which pay dividends back to Social Security for Colas. In this way the Financial Strength of Social Security will always be increasing and the amount paid for Colas will always be increasing. The Funds thus collected and the Securities obtained would be held for the use of social security alone and could not be used by the congress for any other purposes.

For example; the social security tax deduction would be raised by .025 per cent for all workers. Then the monies generated would be used to buy Stocks on the stock exchanges or other securities on other exchanges which would be held in Trust by the Treasury of the United States for Social Security. Only stocks or other securities paying Dividends would be purchased. The Dividends received would then be used as Colas to increase the payouts for each recipient of social security. Eventually enough Dividends would be received; so as to replace the government Colas adjustment and that increase could then be eliminated in favor of the Dividends increase.

In the same way; other government entitlement programs could have a deduction made; which would be used to purchase Securities paying Dividends. The Securities obtained would be held in trust for the particular entitlement program and could not be use by congress for other purposes. The Dividends received would be used to increase the payouts for the particular entitlement program.

This Method would have the end result of strengthening the US Treasury and all of the entitlement programs by means of the value of the securities and would be a method of replacing all of the Colas for the programs with the Dividends received for the securities.

In fact the same method could be used by the Treasury as a means of paying down the national debt...with a percentage of the taxes collected being used to purchase securities to be held in the Treasury to strengthen it; while the Dividends obtained would be used to pay down the national debt. In this way the national debt could actually be reduced to zero!!

Since the government would be purchasing various stocks or other securities for the financial well-being of social security or other entitlement programs; it would be necessary for the government to provide a 'Straw Man' to attend the stockholder or other meetings of these stocks or securities. The Government 'Straw Man' would not normally vote the shares in such meetings....he would just be attending to protect the government's investment in the stock or security.

The government could be limited to a million shares in each stock or security in order to protect the free market for these stocks or securities; if necessary. A US Treasury Committee would meet weekly to determine the government positions in each of the stocks or securities. The government; if it desired to reduce investment in a certain area would try to sell shares in a slow manner so as not to disrupt the normal market. In any case; where the government determined that individuals were trying to 'gut' a company or entity in which the government was invested. The government 'Straw Man' could vote the government's shares against any such proposal in order to protect the government's investment.

Disaster Slab Cities.

Disaster Slab Cities would be set up in fields of states near other states that might have disasters of Tornados or Hurricanes. Thus a Disaster slab city would be set up in Georgia for Florida and a Disaster slab city would be set up in the countryside of Louisiana for New Orleans and in Texas in the countryside for Houston.

A Disaster Slab City would simply be a flat slab of cement in a field with nothing on it except for plumbing, electrical, cable or Wi-Fi, and phone connections. When a Disaster happened ; such as a Hurricane in New Orleans, the government could move tiny mobile houses onto the Disaster Slab City; hook up all of the connections, and then move the people affected by the disaster into temporary government housing there.

Since the slab would ordinarily have no above ground buildings it would not be damaged by Hurricanes or Tornadoes that passed over it before it was utilized. After a severe storm; the government could move in the tiny houses; hook them up, and in no time at all have a functioning little city for the displaced refugees from a disaster in New Orleans or other cities.

Day Care

Companies and Corporations ought to be able to offer Day Care Facilities on their premises with staffing and Facilities that are Tax Deductable. The Day Care Room and its staff's salaries would be Tax Deductable for the Company or Corporation. In this way, working mothers can drop off their kids at the day care at work for free and even visit them at lunch time. Smaller mom and pop shops; say, five of them, can share a convenient day care center for all of them and then each can deduct 20% of the cost of the day care facility and its staff!!

This would provide the working parents peace of mind to have day care for their kids; while at the same time providing a tax deduction for the companies or corporations or small mom and pop stores providing it.

Hospital Staffing and/or Senior Citizen Home or Nursing Home Staffing.

Hospitals, Immediate Care facilities, Nursing Homes, and Senior Citizen homes should be able to deduct the salaries of Doctors, Nurses, and other specialists working for them. In this way; these facilities should never want for having enough staff to cover their patient needs within the Hospital or their Emergency Rooms.

Using this system; you should never find an emergency room that is trying to "get by" with just one of two doctors for a city; but they could have as many doctors on duty as they estimated they would need for worse case scenarios. The same goes for any other immediate care facilities or Nursing Homes or Senior Citizen Homes.

Citizenship and the National Debt.

With the National Debt Ballooning out of Control every year; and Congress Unable to curtail its spending, it's clear that Citizenship can no longer be just given away as some kind of Freebie! A Fee must therefore be assessed for those who want to become Citizens of the United States!!

The Author recommends that people wanting to become Citizens should pay at least $60,000 for the privilege to help pay down the National Debt. This can be deducted from their paychecks by some percentage the same as social security is deducted at present. Fees thus collected would be sent to the US Treasury. Only a Temporary Certificate of Citizenship would be issued until the Fee is paid off. Only after the Fee is paid off would a permanent Certificate of Citizenship be mailed to the recipient. Failure to pay the Fee; after a reasonable amount of time would lead to the revoking of the Temporary Certificate of Citizenship; and the person would then become subject to Deportation again.

In order to pay down the National Debt the author also recommends that a Federal Tax be levied on monies which are wired out of the United States and its Territories to other countries. This could be set at a certain percentage of the funds wired; such as .025 percent. The monies thus collected by the wiring companies would be turned over to the US Treasury and help to reduce our national debt.

Jobs

It should be easy to create necessary jobs in the United States.

Companies and Corporations; in order to foster longevity and stability in the work force, should be able to deduct 1% of the salary of a worker from their taxes per year of employment. Thus after working for a Company or Corporation for a year; the government would allow them to deduct 1% of the salary for that worker the next year. And so on....every year. Thus a Company or Corporation could deduct 50% of the salary of a worker who had worked for them for 50 years from their taxes. This would have the effect of promoting long-term employment and re-training in the workplace for every worker. It would also tend to reduce lay-offs which disrupt the employment and security of the working individual.

Government Initiatives.

One Task that needs to be accomplished is the enhancement and diversification of the US Electrical Grid. The Electrical Grid needs to be Hardened against the Effects of Solar Flares and an EMP ICBM attack against the United States. In addition; the number of self-supporting Electrical Grids need to be increased in the United States. Thus; for instance the City of Washington and the District of Columbia would need to be able to function off either a 'Virginia Grid' or a 'Pennsylvania Grid'. An Electrical Grid in the United States should consist of no more than two or three states and should be able to function independently of the other Grids. This would also prevent really Bad Hurricanes, Tornados, Wind Storms, Blizzards, or other types of destructive storms from bringing down entire sections of the US. In addition; the Cascading effects of sudden power failures or surges which would damage the entire system would be reduced.

Critical Military Resources and Jobs should obviously be kept in the US; rather than relying on foreign and potential enemies as suppliers.....notably China or Russia. Thus Computers, Computer Chips, Hard Drives, Optical Drives, Light Bulbs, cell phones; would all have to have a Domestic production facility protected within the Us and would be forbidden to being purchased by foreign interests which could subvert the intention of these critical industries. Studies should obviously be made to determine which industries are critical or necessary to keep some or all of their production within the US and its territories.

All Houses or Factories being built in the US should be required to have some percentage of photo electric cells on their roof or sides in order to produce some or all of their own energy usage; so as to reduce demand on the local energy grids.

In order to reduce Pollution and traffic grid-lock; the government should encourage more work from home initiatives for the jobs which can do their work over the Internet and/or company Intranet.

A tax reduction incentive could be advanced that a company could deduct the worker's salaries from their taxes for a day for every individual working from home for that day. Of Course; personnel records would have to be kept; so that the government could double-check companies claiming the tax credit.

The Government should also move to start implementing a US wide electrical grid connections for electric vehicles; so that they can be recharged conveniently almost anywhere. This will have the effect of reducing car pollutants and will help in cleaning our air and water. Gas stations could be converted; in part, to re-charging stations with restaurants where people could relax while their cars are being re-charged and/or take electric busses as a side trip to local shops while the car re-charges.

The Government should also be working on a planet wide early warning system for locating asteroids and/or comets which might impact the earth with disastrous consequences. Observatories will have to be set up in all locations possible; such as Easter Island; the Near and Far side of the Moon, etc., so as to provide an early warning system if one is to impact the earth. Probably a nuclear or other small engine type could be used to land on the Asteroid or Comet to 'Nudge' them away from intersecting the earth. Possibly they could be directed into the Sun; so as to be consumed and not to present a threat to the earth again.

The Government should test building houses in a Round Shape in a Tornado or Hurricane prone area to determine if that kind of housing would better withstand the Winds and destructive effects of these kinds of storms. The government could build them and then sell them to prospective buyers at a profit. Then; when storms happened; they would be an automatic study to determine if their survivability was superior to the standard square shape of houses as constructed now. Entire developments could be produced by the government in partnership with a Builder to study these kinds of buildings.

Bicycle sidewalks. In order to accommodate bicyclists; a test city could also try putting in two sidewalks along the roads. The usual 1st sidewalk would be for the pedestrians like now...but the 2nd or inner sidewalk would be for bicyclists. Extra signals might have to be initiated at the intersections; so bicyclists could know when to continue or stop for lights at the intersection. This has the advantage of taking the Bicycles off the roadway for the cars; while at the same time giving the bicyclists a sidewalk or path upon which to move around the city. If the method was put in over an entire city; then it would be possible to Bicycle around the entire city without entering car traffic; except at usual intersections. The extra sidewalk or path would also make it possible for senior citizens utilizing mobile wheelchairs or carts to get around the cities easily, also.

The Unemployed

The Unemployed need to be trained; or re-trained, or enrolled in certification or college degree programs. The Government should provide a barracks for them to live in with a cafeteria for food while they are engaged in taking their training. They can be enrolled in a 'Civilian Conservation Corps' like organization; where they will be required to donate part of their time; when they are not training, in various endeavors to help pay the government back...!! They would be paid a Subsistence level of salary for the part time work; since the government would be providing their housing, food, and some clothes appropriate for the work or training. They could live at the barracks or training facility until they had gotten a job and produced enough income to move out into their own apartments.

The Homeless

For people who are homeless; small communities of the tiny house genre can be set up with plumbing, electricity, phone, etc.; so that people can have a small place to keep themselves safe and off the streets.

It is assumed that people wouldn't want to live there forever; but would act to get training programs in order to better themselves and then move into larger houses for themselves.

These units would be provided for anyone; regardless of age. It would be expected that younger girls and boys; 12 or under years of age would have to be housed in Orphanage-like locations; since they would be considered too young to be on their own.

Groups of children related in the same family; could be kept grouped together in 'Family Rooms' at the Orphanage locations. Or would be allowed to stay together in multi-bed Tiny House Communities.

In this way all of the homeless could be taken off of the streets and made safe during the night. All a person would have to do would be to apply at the facility for a tiny house and it would be provided free of charge for them until they could get a productive job and could move out on their own and get a better apartment.

Bus transportation into town could be provided for the tiny house towns; so that individuals could go apply for work into the cities.

Drug Addiction, Addicts, and Pushers

Drug Addiction would need to have Voluntary sign-Ups for programs and Facilities for people to volunteer to cure themselves of the affects of the Drug Addiction which prevents them from leading normal lives. The government would have to provide these Facilities and Programs.

Drug Addicts; who had become so severely addicted that they had resorted to Crimes to support their habit; would have to be forced to enter a Drug Abuse Program and Housed in Facilities where they would be required to take the Programs to end their Drug addiction. The Government would have to provide these Facilities and Program which would be separate from the Voluntary Facilities and Programs.

Drug Pushers would have to be identified and sentenced to Jail Terms which would be equivalent with the number of people they were supplying drugs to.

Abortion

There may be some justifications for women to get an abortion such as incest, rape, mental deficiency, or inability to care for the child. However; it is also probably true that it is best for the physical, mental and emotional state of the woman to have the baby. The Author is Pro-life ; so he proposes an alternate solution.

The woman has the baby and then gives it up as an Orphan to be raised by the US Government. This gives the baby a chance for life and preserves a citizen for the United States. And it would be terrible for the nation; for instance, to have lost an Einstein, an Edison, an Tesla, or a Hawking to an abortion!

UNITED STATES UTOPIA

(How To Improve and Enhance the United States of America and its Society)

The baby is raised by the US Government in US government Orphanages. When the Orphan reaches the age of 18; he or she is inducted into the armed forces of the US for a period of 10 years in order to pay the government back for raising him. Since the government is providing him with his military clothes, food, and barracks to live in; he is only paid a stipend of; say, the pay rate of the Korean war for his military rank. The current volunteer army would provide the Officers and NCOs of the Orphan army. If and when the orphan re-enlisted; then he would be paid at the volunteer army rate. In no time at all; the United States could have a million men in each of the armed forces.

Any Orphans; when tested, turning out to be geniuses, could be side-tracked into US Government scientific work as a special part of the armed forces, and they would be housed separately from the regular troops.

This solves everybody's problems with abortions and gives life a chance. A Win-Win-Win because the government doesn't lose any geniuses under this plan; and builds up a strong armed forces!

Veterans Administration

The Veterans Administration doesn't have a Funding Problem; it has a Staffing Problem! Basically the VA cannot afford to pay every Doctor the 300,000 a year they think they should be earning. And the VA cannot afford to pay top dollar for Nurses, Technicians, Specialists , or any other kind of Clinicians that it may need.

The only way to adequately staff the VA and Senior Citizen Homes; is with a Selective Service System Draft of the required specialists into the army for a period of six years. A little bit of Discipline and service in the military never hurt anyone by itself; the author is an example of that. Once the individuals are drafted they would be parceled out to the various VA

Hospitals in the continental US and its territories. In the same way senior citizen homes and nursing homes could be staffed with Doctors and Nurses after the needs of the VA are taken care of.

Only the newest graduating class of Doctors, Nurses, Technicians, Physical Specialists, Psychologists, and other types of Clinicians would be drafted and only as necessary to fill the needs and/or vacancies of the VA.

So Doctors and Nurses currently out in private practice would not be affected; only the newest personnel graduated would be subject to the draft. The Draft is necessary; because at present many of the Doctors and Nurses assigned to the VA and Senior Citizen Nursing Homes are not the best Doctors and Nurses; but are the Doctors and Nurses who have seemingly not having been as good in private practice or hospital positions.

The Long Waits for Appointments in the VA would be eliminated; because the VA would have a large supply of drafted Doctors and Nurses to fully staff all of the VA Hospitals and the Senior Citizen Nursing Homes and/or Senior Citizen Homes. The Doctors, Nurses, and Specialists drafted would only serve in the United States and its territories; so career Doctors and Nurses in the armed forces would be freed up to serve overseas.

The Doctors and Nurses would be enlisted into the armed services as officers; much as they are now and would be eligible for veterans benefits after completing their enlistments. In this way part of their cost of medical school could be paid off by the government upon successfully completing their service.

Senior Citizen Homes and/or Senior Citizen Nursing Homes.

Senior Citizen Homes and/or Senior Citizen Nursing Homes would also benefit from this drafting of the newest Doctors, Nurses, etc. as they could be assigned these specialists out of the pool of the l e recruits as soon as the needs of the VA were met.

Police Alternative.

One Alternative the Police might use is the introduction of tranquilizer guns to anesthetize suspects and perpetrators; rather than having to resort to the use of deadly force with a gun. The author realizes that police do not always have the time; when confronting armed suspects, to have the luxury of using a tranquilizer gun on the suspects. The tranquilizer gun could be used on a case by case basis; so as to reduce the number of police shootings. However it is also recognized that this option cannot be used as a criticism against the police, since it is not always possible to utilize it in dangerous situations or where the suspect gives you no time to tranquilize them.

The police do a necessary and heroic job and they deserve to go home at night to their families.

Baby Left in Car Seat Identifier.

This would be a Cell Phone attached to a baby car carrier which would ring or Text or email a parent's cell phone if they had left the weight of a baby in the car seat for over 15 minutes after the car was stopped and forgot the child was in the car for some distracted reason. It would be recharged in a hook up as the baby car carrier was used. In this way it would work to prevent children from being left in hot cars; if the parent had forgot to drop them off at daycare!!

Possible Ideas For the Future.

The Western Union.

The next Evolution of Country-States will probably be the multi-country entity...sort of like the EU has evolved. Thus I recommend that Great Britain, Canada, the United States, Australia, and New Zealand band together for a new kind of union called the Western Union. Each country would still have its current governmental system to elect its President or Prime Minister; but the countries would all be bound together by common international laws and would allow free travel between each of the countries without passports or visas. The new Western Union multi-country would issue its own new Currency called the Western....loosely based on the American

Dollar. It could still have a picture of the Queen of England on the reverse. This would have the advantage of making each individual country stronger....much as each of the states in the United States are made stronger by being part of the United States. It would also tend to reduce differences of opinion and arguments between the member countries and make for a more stable world. Other areas of the world could band together into their own local unions.

The US Petro Dollar.

If the US needed to strengthen its Dollar someday; one possibility is the Issuance of Petro Dollars. That is; each Dollar would be backed by one barrel of oil. So each new Petro US Dollar would be worth roughly $50 or the value of a barrel of oil on the market. Of Course you couldn't pay this off right away; so you would have to make the Petro Dollar only redeemable for oil in ; say, 100 years. You would get an immediate rise in the value of a Dollar; but you would be betting that alternative sources of energy would be found in 100 years and then you wouldn't have to pay off the dollar for oil. The Petro Dollar might start to drive regular federal reserve notes out of the market; but you could set the exchange rate at 500 regular federal reserve notes for one

Petro Dollar. This would slow down any conversions. And each person would be limited to only purchasing 10,000 worth or less of Petro Dollars per year.

Epilogue

A Concise List of the Ideas of United States Utopia.

Abortion. The woman should have the baby and the government raises it as an Orphan. At 18 years of age; the Orphan serves 10 years in the US armed forces to pay the government back ; at the Korean war rates of pay. If the woman insisted she would still have the right of abortion. It is probably Emotionally, Physically, and Mentally better for the pregnant woman to have the baby.

Education. The Government establishes TV Channels and/or websites which allow students to make up courses they need to pass or review. The Government would provide free set-top boxes to log onto the training courses via cable or Wi-Fi and would provide TV screens or other monitors; so the students can take their courses at home. The government would certify the courses and thus students could obtain their GED, Certificates, Bachelor Degrees, and Graduate Degrees at home, if necessary. All subjects would be covered from elementary, Middle, High School, College, and University. Other Courses such as Dancing, Social Graces, Financial Management, etc. would have to be added to the standard school curriculums in order to help the students function in society.

Veterans Administration. The Government should draft the newly Graduating Doctors, Nurses, Technicians, Specialists, Psychologists into the Armed Forces; so as to provide a corps of professionals who can adequately staff the VA Hospitals.

Senior Citizen Homes and Senior Nursing Homes. The Government cans staff these out of the pool of Doctors and Nurses left over from staffing the VA Hospitals.

Digital Bill of Rights. A Digital Bill of Rights should be Amended to the US Constitution. This is to protect Citizen's rights in the Digital Age; something which wasn't imagined by the founding fathers which needs to be addressed. A First Draft of this is provided. It would have to be produced and then submitted to all of the state legislatures to be passed; so it could be added to the US Constitution.

Social Security. Social Security would be provided Financial Stability and an increase in Colas by increasing the SS Deduction by ; say, .025 percent and using the money to buy Dividend paying stocks and other securities. In this way, Dividends paid back to social security would always be increasing and these could be used to supplement Colas and later even replace Colas. The possession of the securities by the Treasury Department would put social security on a firm financial footing. Other US government entitlement programs could be put on a secure financial footing the same way.

Day Care. Companies and Corporations should be able to Deduct a Day Care Room and Staff from their taxes for every facility they set up in all of their factories and work places. In this way free Day Care would be available to every working mother. Small companies could band together in groups

of five to have a local day care; where they could deduct 20% of the cost from their taxes in the same way.

Hospital Staffing. Hospital and Emergency Room Staffing; as well as staffing Immediate Care Facilities and for Senior Citizen Homes and Nursing Homes should be Tax Deductible to the Hospital and other facility. This would have the effect of increasing the number of Doctors and Nurses available at these facilities; so that no Hospital or Emergency Room would be trying to 'scrap by' with just the minimum amount of Doctors and Nurses they would need. The same would go for Nursing Homes and other senior citizen homes. They would be able to increase their staff; as the salaries of these individuals would be tax deductible for them.

Jobs. Companies and Corporations should be able to deduct 1% of the salary of every individual working for it per year. Thus if an individual had worked for a company 51 years; the company would be able to deduct 50% of the individual's salary from their taxes. This is to foster longevity and stability in the workplace and to encourage a company to keep an individual employed. In addition; it would tend to encourage companies to re-train individuals to keep them employed longer at the company.

Government Initiatives. One-Enhancement and diversification of the US electrical grid so that it can withstand an EMP ICBM attack or Solar Flares. This would be implemented by having Local Grids consisting of only a few states each; so an electrical failure event couldn't take down the whole US Grid. Two-A review of Strategic resources and Manufacturing that should be kept operational in the US; so we wouldn't be dependent on foreign resources or production. Three-Most

Houses or Factories built in the US would be required to have some percentage of their electrical usage offset by photo electric cells on their roof or sides. Four-In order to reduce traffic pollution and grid-lock the government should encourage more businesses to let their employees telecommute and work from home. This could be done by the government giving a tax deduction to the company for each employee's salary for the day's worked from home. Five-The Government should immediately start implementing a nation-wide grid of electric re-charging stations for the electrical cars. This would have the effect of reducing pollution and helping clean our air and water. Six-The Government should be setting up a worldwide Asteroid and Comet warning system; so that they can be 'nudged' away from the earth by means of small nuclear or other engines.

UNITED STATES UTOPIA

(How To Improve and Enhance the United States of America and its Society)

The Unemployed. The Government would enroll each unemployed person into a "Civilian Conservation Corps" type of program where they would be housed in Dormitories; fed in Cafeterias, and provided minimum clothing and a subsistence type salary in return for training or certification in a new job and/or taking college courses to receive a degree. For half of their time; they could work in part time government positions in order to pay the government back.

The Homeless. Communities of 'Tiny Houses" could be set up; each with plumbing, electricity, and phone service, etc. which the Homeless could be given free of charge in order to get them off the street and into a safe environment. Buses could be set up to pick them up from the Tiny Home area to take them to training and/or jobs.

Drug Addiction. Free Drug addiction programs would be available for those who have ended up being addicted to one or more types of drugs. Addicts could voluntarily apply to be entered into the free programs. Drug Addicts; who commit crimes, would be offered a choice of jail or a voluntary commitment to a secure drug facility to get them off of their drug addiction. Drug Pushers would be subject to the same punishments and incarceration as now...with their terms of imprisonment equivalent to the number of people they were supplying with drugs!

Citizenship. With the National Debt Ballooning out of control and Congress unable to rein in the spending; Citizenship can no longer be given away as a Freebie! New Citizens would have to pay the US government a Fee for becoming Citizens; something like $60,000 . This fee would be deducted from their paychecks like social security is deducted from paychecks for all citizens. The Funds collected would be sent to the US Treasury to pay down the National Debt. Until the Fee was paid; new citizens would only be given a temporary Certificate of Citizenship. If the Fee was not paid off in a reasonable time; then their temporary certificate would be revoked and they would become subject to Deportation. Paying off the Fee would allow the US Government to mail them a permanent Certificate of Naturalized Citizenship. Monies wired out of the United States to other countries would have to pay a fee of; say .025 percent, and this money generated would be sent to the US Treasury to pay down the National Debt.

Police Alternative. One alternative the police might be able to utilize; in place of the use of deadly force; is the use of tranquilizer guns to anesthetize a suspect or perpetrator. It is recognized that the police in a dangerous situation or in a situation where the perpetrator gives them no time to react; that the police would still have to resort to deadly force to stop the perpetrator.

The Western Union. In the Future; Great Britain, Canada, the United States, Australia, and New Zealand should band together into a new union multi-state like the EU. Each country would retain its present method of electing Prime Ministers or President; but they would be bound together by common international laws and travel would be free of Passports or Visas between them. They would have a new common Currency called the Western; based mostly on the US Dollar. It could still have the picture of the Queen of England on the reverse. Their armed forces and Defense would be integrated together.

The US Petrol Dollar. A possible new US Dollar might be issued backed by a Barrel of Oil; payable in 100 years. This would have the effect of strengthening and raising the value of a Dollar. So as to not drive federal reserve notes out of circulation; the exchange rate would be 500 US Dollars for one Petro Dollar. The US government would be betting that in 100 years an alternate form of energy would have been found and/or the use of oil would have dropped in the future; so that they wouldn't have to pay off the currency in oil.

Meanwhile the US would have enjoyed the rise in the value of the currency.

Disaster Slab Cities. Basically Cement slabs with plumbing, electrical, phone, and cable connections already set up. All that would be needed would be moving the Tiny houses onto it which could be used for refugees from a disaster; such as a Hurricane in New Orleans. The slab cities would not be subject to damage by itself from storms; as it would have no parts above ground. In place of the tiny houses; the government might also use pre-fab warehouse type building setups; which could be setup for the refugees and utilized as long as necessary and then taken down when no longer needed.

Baby Left in Car Identifier. Basically a Cell Phone attached to a Baby Car Carrier which would ring the parent's cell phones and/or Text or email them if the weight of a baby was left in a car seat for more than 15 minutes after the car was parked. This would prevent distracted parents from leaving their kids in a hot car and forgetting them for some reason.

About the Author

Merrell D. Wilson is a Military Historian and a Strategic Analyst and Strategic Gamer.

He Served in the United States Regular Air Force during the Vietnam War.

He is named after General Merrill of Merrill's Marauders of World War II Fame.

His Sister Glenna; was partly named after the B-24 Bomber; the Glenna Bea, her relative flew in during WWII for 40 missions in the Pacific theatre.

Merrell D. Wilson is also Author of "The Correct Military Strategy For the Vietnam War".

UNITED STATES UTOPIA

(How To Improve and Enhance the United States of America and its Society)

Made in United States
Orlando, FL
05 November 2026

90230226R00052